Minnesota
Land of 10,000 Lakes

Tika Downey

PowerKiDS press.

New York

Published in 2010 by The Rosen Publishing Group, Inc.
29 East 21st Street, New York, NY 10010

First Edition

Editor: Joanne Randolph
Book Layout: Kate Laczynski
Book Design: Greg Tucker
Photo Researcher: Jessica Gerweck

Photo Credits: Cover © SuperStock/age fotostock; p. 5 Ryan/Beyer/Getty Images; p. 7 David Boyer/ National Geographic/Getty Images; pp. 9, 13 Paul Chesley/Getty Images; pp. 11, 15, 15 (inset), 17, 19, 22 (monarch, loon, flower) Shutterstock.com; p. 22 (tree) © www.istockphoto.com/Alexey Sokolov; p. 22 (F. Scott Fitzgerald) Hulton Archive/Getty Images; p. 22 (Walter Mondale) Douglas Graham/ Congressional Quarterly/Getty Images; p. 22 (Charles Schulz) Cindy Charles/Getty Images.

Library of Congress Cataloging-in-Publication Data

Downey, Tika.
   Minnesota : Land of 10,000 Lakes / Tika Downey. — 1st ed.
      p. cm. — (Our amazing states)
   Includes index.
   ISBN 978-1-4358-9354-2 (library binding) — ISBN 978-1-4358-9804-2 (pbk.) — ISBN 978-1-4358-9805-9 (6-pack)
   1. Minnesota—Juvenile literature. I. Title.
   F606.3.D694 2010
   977.6—dc22
                                        2009027399

Manufactured in the United States of America

CPSIA Compliance Information: Batch #WW10PK: For Further Information contact Rosen Publishing, New York, New York at 1-800-237-9932

Contents

Land of 10,000 Lakes

Minnesota is often called the Land of 10,000 Lakes. It actually has at least 12,000 lakes. If you visited one lake each day, it would take almost 33 years to visit them all! The lakes helped give the state its name. The name "Minnesota" comes from a Native American term that means "sky-**tinted** waters."

Minnesota is along the northern border of the United States. Around it are North Dakota, South Dakota, Iowa, Wisconsin, and Lake Superior, one of the **Great Lakes**.

The state is famous for its forests and beauty as well as its lakes. It also has the famous Mayo Clinic, where doctors help sick people from around the world.

4

Kabetogama Lake is part of northern Minnesota's Voyageurs National Park. The park is known for its waterways, which were once used by fur traders.

Once Upon a Time in Minnesota

Minnesota's first people arrived at least 10,000 years ago. These people were **ancestors** of the Chippewas, Sioux, and other Native Americans. Some of them cut pictures called **petroglyphs** into rocks. You can still see the petroglyphs in places throughout the state.

French and English fur traders began arriving around 1660. The United States claimed the land in 1783 and began building **Fort** Snelling in 1819.

Minnesota became a state in 1858. However, there were problems between settlers and Native Americans. In 1862, the Sioux attacked settlers and started a war. Many Sioux left or were killed. The rest were moved to **reservations** in other states.

A Chippewa girl looks at carvings on some rocks near Nett Lake. Nett Lake is on the Bois Forte Reservation, in northern Minnesota.

Land, Lakes, and More

Long before people arrived, sliding **glaciers** shaped Minnesota's land. They dug low areas that filled with water to form the state's famous lakes. They created small hills, deep valleys, and plains in central and southern Minnesota. They formed rocky hills and mountains in the north. That is where you find Eagle Mountain, Minnesota's highest point, and Red Lake, its largest lake. Lake Itasca, where the mighty Mississippi River begins, is there, too.

The Mississippi is not Minnesota's only important river. The Minnesota River, St. Croix River, Rainy River, Red River of the North, and St. Louis River all cut through Minnesota's land, too. Some rivers have waterfalls. One of the most beautiful is Minnehaha Falls.

A barge passes some Minnesota factories on the Mississippi River. The Mississippi, which starts in Minnesota, is one of the longest rivers in North America.

Weather and Wild Things

Minnesota has cool to warm summers and cold, snowy winters. Northeastern Minnesota gets about 6 feet (2 m) of snow yearly!

All sorts of plants and animals live in Minnesota. Forests cover one-third of the state. Wildflowers, berries, and grasses grow there, too. There are big animals like deer, bears, elk, moose, and gray wolves, and small animals like porcupines and woodchucks. Songbirds, hawks, eagles, and owls also live there. One special bird is the common loon, Minnesota's state bird.

The common loon looks somewhat like a large, black-and-white duck with a pointed bill. It can dive very deep to catch fish. It is known for the strange laughing sound it makes.

The common loon is built for swimming and does not go on land often. It eats its food under water, and its bill has sharp parts for holding on to fish.

Farms, Forests, and Factories

Have you eaten carrots, peas, potatoes, corn, or apples lately? They might have come from Minnesota farms. You might have had food sweetened with sugar from Minnesota sugar beets. Your breakfast eggs, milk, and Thanksgiving turkey might have come from Minnesota, too.

Minnesota's factories make many goods. Forests supply wood for paper and special building boards. Farms supply corn for ethanol, which is mixed with gasoline. Factories also make computer goods and tools for treating sick people.

Many big companies have **headquarters** in Minnesota. Some of these companies are Target, Best Buy, and General Mills, which makes many types of foods including breakfast cereal.

This Minnesota farm is using contour farming and strip cropping to keep water from running away from crops that are planted on a hill.

The Twin Cities

St. Paul, the state capital, is in southeastern Minnesota on the eastern bank of the Mississippi River. Across the river is Minnesota's largest city, Minneapolis. Together, they are called the Twin Cities.

St. Paul began as a small settlement called Pig's Eye. Today, visitors come to see old **mansions** and **museums**, such as the Minnesota History Center and the Science Museum. The yearly St. Paul Winter Carnival has a **contest** for ice and snow **sculptures**. The yearly Aquatennial includes boat races and a sand castle contest!

Minneapolis's name means "water city." It comes from the Sioux word *minne*, which means "water," and the Greek word *polis*, which means "city."

14

Minnesota's capitol, in St. Paul, opened in 1905. *Inset:* Minneapolis's Stone Arch Bridge, once a railroad bridge, is now used for biking and walking.

Spoonbridge and Cherry

Can you imagine a 52-foot (16 m) spoon with a cherry on top? In Minneapolis, you do not have to imagine it, you can see it! A famous sculpture by Claes Oldenburg and Coosje van Bruggen, called *Spoonbridge and Cherry*, serves as a fountain in the Walker Art Center's sculpture garden. It took three years to complete the sculpture. The 11-acre (4 ha) sculpture garden is the nation's largest urban sculpture park. There are more than 40 works that are always there and many sculptures that come for a short stay.

The sculptures are not the only thing to see at the Walker Art Center. The Walker Art Center has interesting artwork inside its walls, too. Be sure to stop by when you are in Minneapolis!

Spoonbridge and Cherry is meant to get people talking and thinking about art. What do you think about when you look at it?

Split Rock Lighthouse

Lake Superior, which touches northeastern Minnesota, is famous for its lighthouses. In the late 1800s and early 1900s, many ships carried goods across the lake. Strong winds and high waves put the ships in danger, so the U.S. government built lighthouses along the shore to help guide the ships. Minnesota's famous Split Rock Lighthouse operated on its shore from 1905 until 1969.

For a long time, life at the lighthouse was hard and lonely. For 15 years, it could be reached only by boat, so few visitors came and the lighthouse keeper's family would visit only in the summer. In the 1920s, a road was built that connected the lighthouse to the mainland. Today many people visit the lighthouse to learn about its history.

Though Split Rock Lighthouse is no longer a working lighthouse, the light is sometimes turned on as part of a celebration of its history.

Minnesota State Symbols

State Tree
Norway Pine

State Butterfly
Monarch

State Flag

State Bird
Common Loon

State Flower
Pink and White
Lady's Slipper

State Seal

Famous People from Minnesota

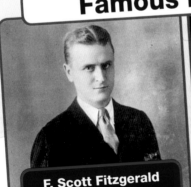
F. Scott Fitzgerald
(1896–1940)
Born in St. Paul, MN
Author

Walter Mondale
(1928–)
Born in Ceylon, MN
U.S. Vice President

Charles M. Schulz
(1922–2000)
Born in Minneapolis, MN
Cartoonist

22

Minnesota State Map

Minnesota State Facts

Nicknames: The Land of 10,000 Lakes, The North Star State,
The Gopher State

Population: 5,220,393

Area: 86,280 square miles (223,465 sq km)

Motto: "L'Étoile du Nord" ("The Star of the North")

Song: "Hail Minnesota," by Truman E. Rickard and Arthur E. Upson

Index

Web Sites

Due to the changing nature of Internet links, PowerKids Press has developed an online list of Web sites related to the subject of this book. This site is updated regularly. Please use this link to access the list:

www.powerkidslinks.com/amst/mn/